Words Without End. By Judith J. Willis

Copyright © August 31, 2019 by Judith J. Willis

All rights reserved.

Formatting and Editing by Judith Willis

Copyright © 2019 by Judith J. Willis

Words Without End © by Judith J. Willis

Cover by Chanice Gray

No part of this book may be reproduced.

In any form without the written

Permission of the Author Judith Willis

Self- Published in Canada by Judith J. Willis

Picture on back cover by Rosemary Lamon

Words Without End. By Judith J. Willis

ISBN 978-1-9990228-2-2

$12.50 CAN

WORDS WITHOUT END

GARRETT AND ROXANNA 89-90

Oh, what weary roads we travelled, be still my beating heart,

calm sway across the room your love awaits

Time again the merry-go-a-round

Life calm imperfect the heart, we will defeat and walk away with

smiles. Comes to me with twilights, comes away there is still

wars to won. Wars with guns and chains, wars with flying fists

and venomous words. Come my love conquer or lost, the

chapter is here, it is clear. Meets with will of chains, feet planted

firm. Mark the line you wish me not to crossed because in your

path broken glass. Spin your tales history is here. Make me

weep! Garrett, with his fearless and possessive heart makes me

weep no more, if I have my husband the world holds my highest

regards. I snuggled deep into the arms of my love and my love;

my heart is truly complete. If you never known love, it will never

know you, embrace it, do not let fear be your guide. Listen to

the beats of hearts. It will recognize the rhythm; be insight and it

will land softly within your path.

Oh! Love the wonder, the splendor of being in love. A song, a

song to sing with joyous heart and a tongue to speak, walk

flowing.

Oh! The grander of love overflowing with harmony.

KEEP

I want to marry you in that black dress, that

always hang in the closet that be friend cobwebs

and spiders it is perfect to set the mood right

My visit to the other side

Absent with feeling words could not define

Wanting blood bleeding, bringing me to my knees

For sleep will not come easily

I burn bridges to escape what I witness

Wait for me on the promenade

I cannot believe my eyes the bleak blue sky

You come out of the grave burning fire,

cannot diminish,

Me on the other side

Promises kept

Secret hold

Take it to the grave!

The vortex

YOURS

A memory, a touch who would of recognize

love

A kiss is still a kiss but kissing you brings magic

and mystery

Each night I closed my eyes, I cannot wait to see

what mystery unfold

I love you in the deep blue

I cannot solve the mystery of being yours

I wage wars to hold on a bit more

My beautiful body of wine

My siren in the deep blue sea

I will live on cotton candy and popcorn

If all it takes to continuing being yours

A million touch, I will wait for you at the edge of

the void to kiss your feet

Promises is bliss, I will watch as tear fall from

the sky

DEEP BLUE

Your strength lifts me up!

I do not know how my fall splattered, if your arms

wouldn't break my fall,

The look in your eyes searching for reason why,

Every story has a beginning and an end

Take me to the moment when mystery no longer

hold hope,

What unfold to make you want to give end to life?

Who shut doors to reason to end?

Your love is the ocean, calm and beautiful,

The next raging, erupted volcano

Where passion meet, I am a man on my knees,

The heaven shake wanting, calm beautiful seas,

Thunder and lighting are never my mistake to kiss

cheek when heaven meet.

WISH

If you were my Genie in a bottle

Would you grant me just one wish?

To make this cease never to exist!

To never taste your kisses

If I never remove my armor cut would never

bleed

Heart will never break.

Trust would never be questioned.

Your accomplishment from the start went.

Straight to the heart

SO LONG

It been so long,
So long since you hold my hand,
It been so long since that midnight dance,
So long, so long since a man show me how to slow
dance,
So long, so long, so long
I forgot how to slow dance,
Since you kiss me in the barn at the brink of dawn
Did we even have a chance?
So long, so long
Baby show me how to slow dance,
Baby dim the light,
Come and whisper to me,
Bang, bang come and bring it home,
Light the candles,
Kiss me here, come and do me right here,
Baby put out my fire.

WRECKED

I am a man,

I am the disease,

I will wrecked, and watch you bleed.

I the disease the world need

My face, you will see as the breeze whispered

haunted secrets,

See triumphs, trials, enter my domain,

I am the worst enemy,

The disease that meant to be

You try to have control over me,

But I am here to stay,

This is your faith,

FEAR

I never grasp that I love you ,

Until I hear the echoes of the door closing

The final moment

What was right before me,

It was not the fear of you finding someone more

desirable,

Or the fear of dying or watching the world burn,

Or the sound of your laughter

Or that you will never be mine again

The very thoughts that I will never lay eyes upon

your face,

This is my biggest fear,

LOVE

Darling come kiss your bride to be,

I have waited a lifetime for this to be!

Run kisses along cheek,

Come make body mold,

Come make heart race,

Thunder and lighting breaks

Come set worlds aflame,

Come bade in the sunlight of my craze,

Come to me in the after glow

Come put out flaming fire,

Come sooth shiver, come sooth desire,

Come dance at dawn, the touch of twilight,

Come before sleep wake me from heartbeats,

MY LIFE

Stumbling in the dark drunkard

Trying to understand or find reason,

Why life cannot be,

Waking up in puke and vomit

Cannot understand defeat,

Continuing to disgrace good name with fail

inventions,

Waking near dumpster

Try, try,

Fail, fail,

I will rise beyond this world,

Thereafter, if nothing but being brave

TWILIGHT

Comes, to me in the mid of twilight,

Comes, thus come a thousand time,

Come walk the path along me,

Come this is the moment to be,

Eternity!

I'll will wait,

Absent hearts beats,

Slipping into insanity,

Darling, where the life you promised me?

NOT ME

Bade in your kiss, shadows,

I imagined this!

The softness of your kiss

The touch of your caress

All this, I imagine!

What do I……

The mist of shadow of your kiss?

Come back, moment to escape,

What could be warm embrace?

Lips like steel soft when touch by me,

Melt me, make this real

ASHES

Arise, arise cast me from sight!
Look not upon me, there is no mirror that would
accept me!
For in the dark corners, I am one with thee,
There are no loving arms reaching out to mold me,
I have accepted my faith! Bore from love, arise
from hate,
I am which you crave,
I am what the darkness mold, the darkness
embrace,
For I look into your eyes, into the void,
And see what must be, what I am to be,
Arise from cocoon, investigate the plague I will be
Chaos you will marry me!
For I see through the vale, my eyes are no longer,
blind for now I have eyes to see,
We must all embrace what we will truly be,
Arise from ashes, arise from dusk, arise!

NEVER

I will never know your lips,

Never know warm embraces,

A million smiles, a million crimes

A million-sunrises,

Slowly I rise, slowly I go insane,

Slowly I die

I am me no more,

I spy the clay doll that which I was bore,

I breathe as you see life, the breath in me,

As I become the clay now lay scattered on the

sidewalk for the world to see

FOUL

Foul disposition,

Shut your mouth,

stop spreading poison,

Every word out of your lying mouth is toxic!

Your clothes are venom, lies and chaos grown on

you like vines!

Madness see no reasons to cry,

Cry, cry, I laugh you hide,

Cold heart does not bleed!

Frozen in time cease to exist,

Embrace shackled in chain,

Into the abyss

CONFINEMENT

Cage, cage I miss your warm embrace,
Tied me up, chain me to the dungeon wall,
For I missed the warm embrace of metal,
Clinging to my chain for warm embrace,
The light from the sunlight blind my eyes,
For I miss the prison in the sky,
Cockroaches and Mice visit me in the limelight,
I fail to understand human emotions,
Years in my cage has left me numb,
When your eyes smile, I see demon behind your
eyes,
My claws come out shrinking behind invisible cage,
For in panic, take me back shrinking in my cage,
Calm, stillness as I watch the waves in the ocean,
Afraid as heart race, as the clouds changes shapes,
Unicorn and Elves look down what is now me,
Unrecognized beauty is she!

RESCUED

Cover me if you see me bleeding,

Cover me if you find me in an alleyway naked,

Cover me, if you see battered and bruises,

Would you stop fists raining down on me?

Feet stomp in defeat,

Witness come forth; you murder me!

You, shy away,

 You thy witness,

Guilty, as thee,

The weapon is not fist nor feet,

Live in fear of falling fists,

This is how life must end for me,

 It is that you refuse to acknowledge or rescue me!

NEVER MEANT TO BE

No matter how hard I try, I cannot understand reason

why you refuse me!

The tear fall to ocean stream; years has gone by,

 Why my heart still crave you like a theft in the night.

Love betray like fool's games; I have not closed thy

eyes since what I thought could be beautiful melodies,

Nothing but heartache and broken memories

 Tears will not stop falling, body do not witness me

crawling under my rock I shrink away,

The hate that you show, fangs away.

 Shattered to ashes and dusk, for once I thought I

know and recognize you,

What master you must be to make believe what meant

to be to a fool like me!

UNRECOGNIZE

Arise, arise see claws that is now eyes,

I dream of you last night!

I cry what I cannot imagine before my eyes,

Jealous make you feel that you now recognize,

Alas, arise come to me with unicorn as through

breeze,

Come thus a thousand time before,

Lay claim if truth, not fantasy,

Arise, arise,

In death, in life,

This marriage cannot take place,

For in death you must now accept, to reborn!

I cannot claim you even in death!

For you must undistorted, this is the reality,

This death!

CALLING

Abide, true as light awake me from sleep!

For darkness is light, come truth, come light,

For I see sleep brought me forth light,

In confusion that is thy mind, for I cannot

understand,

Why darkness call me forth that is night.

For in dream that is life,

For you seek me out which that is night,

Make reason know why you haunt beauty that is

sleep.

For as, I awake from slumber, which meant for

rest,

Haunted and hazy, what is this meaning?

For I feel I am duress!

CYPHER

Symbol, symbol I know thee, words fail to voice,

Atop the world amongst the trees,

Symbol on sand, you float before me!

Cypher, meaning of being,

What does it mean as you bow down before me?

Speak, as thus speak a thousand time,

Unscramble speak your truth!

For a thousand years you stood before me!

Make known cypher, riddles, symbols,

Riddled me this, riddle me that,

Crack the code and let it be known.

The meaning of life,

Symbols in riddles throughout times

PRETTY THINGS

Rainbow colours, pretty colours, pretty things

Frills and fringe, color, and candies

Pretty birds soaring this way and that way,

Firecrackers and rainbow in the sky,

Raindrop and waterfall see animals and creeks,

Forest and trees, mystery,

Pretty things, frills, and things

ECHO

Hollow inside, same dreams, same page in the book,
Cannot get pass what I didn't took, page three I
read hundred of time, page four is waiting for
hundred of years,
This emptiness, this hollowness!
Where did it come from?
When it starts, to live without cause!
Accomplish nothing to get nothing,
To be passing memories, to hold no ground, no
roots,
In space floating without a destination,
Lost in limbo trying to find place where accepted,
understand being, who am I?
Unclaimed property in lost and found,
Travel world, travel time, understand,
I am in the same spot,
I 'm always behind, not detained never forward,
Secret of life enjoy moments as if there where
your last. Grasping as straws and clouds,
In vapor lost,
Forgotten like mist in fogs,
Echo in distance fading,
Echo in beat of drums.
Echo lost,

LOSS CAUSE

Masked!
Afraid? I feel your eyes on me, chilling my bone
with stares,
I stand at the corner of the highway,
They do not want to see, if they did, they would
stop!
You would think! Hours as the rain pour down on the
soulless sinner sin. Masks we all wear to hid what
we truly are,
Rattle snakes in wool clothes, as the dark reveal
itself,
Crawl on me worms! As if the cold of the rain is all
I need,
Steer my blood, the hour is near the blackness will
pass again, I left wondering what fear I will
unfolded?
Creep on me make skin crawl,
Waking with blood on thy hands, for as I look in
the mirror, I see no one there. For as I am,
screaming the mirror hold no reflection or specter,
I look in the blackness, as sure as I removed the
mask unwilling to accept I,
I 'm unmasked!

ONE KISS

Imagine your kiss, drinking from your lips,

Aahh, I would imagine we will make it like this,

laying on the beach in magic and bliss,

just from one kiss!

With more kisses, would you take me like this?

 Let me forget that this world exist!

I am burning with elevate anticipation,

I 'm lost in rapture of hidden fear!

What are you waiting for?

Kiss me!

Help me escape my gilded cage,

One kiss.

I know you would move me like this!

EMPTY HAND

Escaping what is in the mirror is like running

away from shadows,

seagull in flight,

The crow of roosters,

A new day, a new dawn, a new battle, won or lost,

Arise from sweet sleep, meet the world amongst

the heap, reaped, reaped,

 strip me to skin and bone,

Strip me to my knees!

Make me weep,

Make me weep, I will show no mercy,

I will cut and make you bleed.

FIX

Counting backward from one hundred, as the

antiseptic take effect. I feel the knife as it

slices through me. Four times you try to perfect

what is damage within me ,

How many more before you will accept,

What is broken is meant to be,

Thy faith is seal,

Broken battered bruised,

Here I stand before you!

For blood is thicker than skin,

I hide away in corners, my hiding places,

My solace, choked on my shame,

Hide in disgrace,

You take away what was once grace,

Shame me, I shrink away left to rot,

Until you find purpose, reason to exist once

more,

SUMMONED

I summoned thee to breathe, to take life,

To give life, to have life, I bless thee,

I call to thee with three gold coins from ancient

time,

To have three life, on bended knee,

I summoned thee to breathe,

I beg thee, I command thee, come forth as this

candle burn low,

Take life that I bid thee,

Come forth to me,

I summoned thee!

Blessed be,

WAIT

A single candle leave burning on the porch each

night,

Like a beacon,

To be your guide home,

Waiting for return,

Waiting for fulfilled promises keep,

Waiting for my man,

Waiting to fall asleep.

WEEP

Ashes weep for me no more, you witness,

Shamed, all my tears,

You know hidden fear, weep no more,

Lesson learn, grow up big and bold ashes resend,

God witness,

I try to find peace,

trying to sleep, but you haunt me!

You reach your hand out, captured by the wind,

Heaven know I try to be a good girl, but you tied

me up in chain and make me a prisoner to unseen

crime,

Restless night I hear cries,

trumpets and horns,

My hand above my eyes

Coiled,

Released me from thy mortal shackled!

GARDEN

I would sit,

I would listen to birds singing,

Butterfly fluttering wings

Serene fragrance I can no longer tolerate,

Sneezes and hives that is my wills,

 If I choose to sit and tolerate what was once

majestic

Witness rebirth as bloom and blossom enter

anew stage in life,

Caged cornered,

APPEARED

Angel of Death, here on earth!

Faith and understanding,

You brought hope with faith,

Accept me!

I cannot be sway!

This is your time!

Take my hand!

Accept defeat!

This is your time come with me!

Of that sweet way I was into despair!

What say you now? What comfort have we now?

By heaven, I will hate him everlastingly.

Richard the Second. Shakespeare

CLEAR

It's crystal clear, shadows,

I do not appear even when I hear thy name,

Whispering in the wind,

You disappear, it clears I am not here,

Into shadow,

I 'm comfortable being shadow,

 In my mirror,

 I sees how,

I appear.

MEMORIES

You got your hook in me like a puppet on a string, your
hold on me clawing in skin, I cannot breathe.
I pray the Lord to give me strength.
Not a day goes without seeing your face. I am trap in
these memories, cannot move forward, time has stood
still,
Your hook in me is deep, I try to resist, you my con
artist, caught like a fly in a trap, there is no place to go,
no hiding place. I move mountain but your hook in me
woven deep into my soul, going insane by the hour,
I wait for your return.
Lord give me strength I am losing my mind trying to get
you outta my soul is like imprinted tattoo scarring my
heart, waiting for wound to heal is an impossible feat.
I been into the shadow, this is my moment to shine
hallelujah!
I am dying slowly like leaf falling from trees, my body
wither up like prune, loving a man like you. I cannot
explain why my heart doesn't move on and accept
defeat.

SORROW

Do not let me drown in sorrow,

Do not let me drown in pain,

Tomorrow, tomorrow if tomorrow comes dawn,

Will drowned out sorrow and brings forth no

more pain,

Lost in shadows of thoughts,

Watching the snow fall, match the coldness,

Morbid of my heart.

Flutter away,

Sorrow, sorrow wash away,

On the morrow,

Recapture and bring forth thy soul!

LOOK

When I look at you, I see heaven!

What I imagine would be the stars above my head,

walking on clouds,

Oh! What melodies as I walk toward you my sweet

hereafter

Hope is a dangerous thing, to want what outta

reach.

In wonder

What it meant to be in your arms.

Held after the storm every moment in your present

left me breathless,

I watch from a distance; she doesn't love you like I

do!

I will climb mountains swim across oceans to

catches a glimpse of you!

Watching as your back walking away from me.

DARK CREATURE

I dream the dream that is nightmare,
But are you real? Before my eye beautiful creature
My heart stumble, you compelled me!
While you circled, mercy me.
Creature of my mind, wait awhile, my mind,
behold you, my eyes, cold, cold inside creature of my
mind. Nightmare I have created,
Eyes deceived me, are you real dream?
Between the lashes I see hoofs and heels,
My heartbeat faster as you breathe,
Creature crawling on wall,
Come to me slowly, I'm not afraid!
My tremor is not fear,
Embrace, while I hold you close,
Mobile, creature of night,
Crawl on me, blood run cold,
Crawl on skin I feel the sparks,
Open yourself to me!
Slowly, slowly, breathe as I catch my breath,

creature into the dark, take my hand.
I promise I wouldn't bite. I wait for the moment,
Beautiful creature, I watch as you disappear before my
eyes, this can't be real!
Creature, creature of my dream,
I will not laugh; I bow down on my knees.   *Cont.......*

Begging you please. Alone! Cold!
At least, now I have purpose.
Here in the dark, shadow on the wall.
Please let me in, I walk, and I walk and wonder,
What my mind refuses to voice.
I am not alone, at last! Years I dream of you, hoping my mind will not bleed out. Crawling, crazy I dream you! But you are just shadow of some wild imagination., I dream you up. Wanting, wanting to hold straws alone.
I stood watching worlds fade. Dark creature I faded into thin air, calling to dusk into thin air. The shadow has no one, touching shadows my magician is catching the dark unaware! The feather touch of hands, the touch of insanity. Shadow consume me. You the touch of light, radiance. On the back of a stallion, you swoop me higher. Shadows, creature of the night walking backward. My illusions don't falter. The night run into nowhere circling in circles. You get nowhere, howls, screams blood run deep. Frozen in stance shadows my dark. Crawl on skin, awake or sleep you compelled me! Embrace that you crave the dark, light out. Floating in midair, creature where did you go to? Doubt, my fear falter. It's 3 am I'll stay until light find way into the shadows, dark, dark come to me! Blood run deep; the dark evolves me! The mystery of the dark,
The crack of dawn see life fresh start.   Cont.....

Swifter paralyze take a moment, release, released me
from deep sleep, arms trying to enfold me.
Fear crippled me! Reaching in mind the clash of Titans.
Timeless evolve into shadow then dusk no more breath
stillness, nightmare is real, step into the parlour stay
awhile, in the dark shadows move, crimson the smell of
tulips, wilted, lifeless silence nowhere and here.
Silence is a deadly thing, as I watch worlds.
 Shadow reaching out in the dark, shock to the system
compelled me to see, yeah, reaching out through the void,
Where the light through the dark!
Retrace steps, blinded to see shadow dancing in the
dark.
Imagine a steep cup of tea, savour the stillness why
darkness evolves into darkness. While heartbeats, Body
shivered. Race you here and there.
Reach nowhere. Garden, garden of Eden.
Fountain of youth. Ageless time a touch of light feather
fluttered,
Circle back to you, dreams of dream screamed.

ALONE NEAR

Here I sat alone as days roll into years.

Alone, alone I can't see clear.

I can feel the chill in my bone as the sound of the wind

howled, the hour draw near, and you never did appear.

I can't say I am disappointed; moments were brief,

you hold me dear.

Inside, inside I crumble and hide fear.

Here I am, survive this last dance!

Before I meet the maker, at last shadow and mirror

roll into mirage and now, I understand I was chasing

shadows,

The moon and stars can live near without burning each

fear.

Thunder and lighting crashing as dawn draw near.

Here alone, I stand behold this beautiful sunset.

I laugh, I still want you here, madness that is mine.

Beautiful mirage at last, I see clear.

NIGHT AND DARK

Night and dark you are the same,

Light and shadows,

I screamed out loud as my lung carry,

What I' m living for? If not alone!

Rain falling. Distance as the ocean waves

Here on the board walk left with memories and music,

memories of my muse, shock to the system,

Cruel to love without love and walk into mist where there

is no light and wondering into the dark,

Blinded by the dark circling like vultures waiting for

feast.

You are stronger than imagine, wait for the shock to

falter! Come into the light from the shadows streaming

to the moon and wait on the beach till noon from the

dark, there is brilliance light captured by Picasso,

Dark here is night You that survive, and you that sleep *in*

fame!

EYES

Give me eyes,

Eyes to see beautiful body,

Hand, hand to feel,

Flowing, air to breathe,

Whispering to me,

Caressing like the wind,

I wanna be near you!

Cry's, heaven is you tonight,

Flowing,

Caressing,

Hearst beats,

Let me run my hand through your hair,

Come closer, be inside,

Slide, flowing,

Heaven, eyes on you,   Cont......

I wanna move.

Silky, Smokey like the wind blows,

I need to feel what you promised,

Rides, wind blowing,

Heaven, I wanna be near you!

I can feel you near!

Hand like fire,

Slide like the tide,

I wanna feel, come closer,

Ride like the tides,

 blows my mind,

Slow, slowly you on my mind,

I wanna cry, heaven eyes on you tonight,

Smile, cries

This is my ride, hearts break, crack ice,

Hand like fire.

HOPE

I walk the street in hunger I follow the path of chaos,
My limb feels the hunger and stumbles.
Park cars north, I see hope and a touch of awe,
Outreach arms and stumble. Hope is gone!

Death is knocking at my door!

Not ready to go Lord! Show me the ways to salvation!

Blackness enfold me as I stumbled.

These streets are for heroes, this is no way for Angels
to fly home. Echoes of footstep as my eyes fluttered
open. I know I am not in Heaven; I still feel your
presence while you watch over me,

This is where uneven path and rocky road has led me.

Wake up trapped in chains, a ray of light at the back
of my eyes, voices whispering what is to become of me.

 All hope is gone but fear live on

My belly no longer feel hunger,

A new hope, a new dawn, a touch of hope lingers,

YOU

You got this rhythm about you!

Heads turned,

The world wants to meet you,

Magic and mystery,

You are not mine to keep,

Heart break, heartache,

The prize is with you tonight,

You set flames along paths,

The way you undress with your eyes,

The way you move, my mind is crashing in overdrive,

You got me tied up in knot,

Blues and mystery

THE FALL

The fall from design

The fall of desire

The virgin falls,

Heart breaks

Hope fall, man on it knees,

No ordinary love

Bare feet walking

Broken glasses

This is the fall, how man crumbled!

FOR SALE

I refuse to let you use my blackness against me,

you see me as a threat. Because I am black!

Do you need to cut in front of me in the lineup?

You did not see me standing there?

I am not ashamed of being black!

You never let me forget it, you remind me every day,

When you spit at me when you kick me.

When you call me monkey!

You do not see a girl in front of you!

You see a threat, why? Because I am different

Do, I not bleed red like you?

Do I not cry when I am sad?

You think you are inferior?

When I speak my mind, you hold your grudge against

me!

I will not be silence; I held my tongue long enough!

Before you use your superpower for good, you use for

evil.   Cont....

We will never move forward if you do not see me or

recognize that I am here to stay!

I am not just a number or a dollar sign!

I decide my own faith,

Rather than applauding me for speaking up, to speak my

mind. You turn back,

You serve me further injustice,

Double deal, double talking like a drug dealer,

Words that cannot be trust, words without end.

Mean what you say! And do what you mean!

The system never changes if you hide behind words,

Words without meaning,

Empty lifeless words,

Everyone is for sale if the price is right!

You hide behind badge and shield!

What your price?

GUN FOR HIRE

What? do you think gonna happen with the gun in
hands? You shot me dead on the ground!
The wail of the siren, hasten stride,
This is how you explain being a man?
You would not let me go, now I'm dead on the
ground.
This is not a crime of passion, if it happens only in
your mind, the cop is hunting you gun for gun, what
does it matter in your get-a-way speeding car.
When you break out in cold sweat,
An eye for an eye only happens when you commit a
crime. Don't you wish me here now? But you gunned
me down dead on the ground, wish you hate me
now? Gun for hire, you are a big man now. You take
life for fame living underground the party of five,
one grand for chain, two for nail, three for visual
limbs confirmation, four for tortured, five to take
lives that makes up the party of five, gun for hire.

No, I will speak as liberal as the north:
Let heaven and men and devils, let them all,

All, all cry shame against me, yet I'll speak.

Othello. Shakespeare

WARRIORS

I pack up my sword and shield I'll repent my sin if
need be,
I'll stop fighting wars if you'll find your way to me,
I'll travel through time ready for war at your
command,
Ready for war, ready for war,
I see you cruising through the street leaving blood in
your wake trying to find me, when all you need to do
is get down on your knees, praising hallelujah,
Trying to find me, trying to find me,
Take up the gun, look to me from medieval time to
Mohmmad Ali,
  When the words of a knight, will make you sleep at
  night, honour, respect duty above all to protect
  thee!
  I put down my machine gun and praise the Lord,
  Mother Mary!
    Ready to war.

ECHOES 11

Echoes of empty space

Echoes of memories

Echoes of the drums, the sound of my heart

Echoes of silence,

Echoes of memories lost,

After the storm, there is no calm

Echoes, echoes the sound on the other side of

the bed,

Echoes lost,

Echoes the sound my heart makes,

Untraceable lost,

Echoes in movement,

Echoes of clouds,

Echoes lost.

RETURNED

My heart weep for you, the love you didn't returned.

My body cry out to you into the void.

Not even water could quench the thirst that woven so

deep,

What could never be the love you make me see.

I fell asleep,

As I watch you put one foot in each pant on the beach,

Centuries pass and still my heart will not understand,

We were strangers in the night. Comes away,

Weep no more,

Memories are forever,

Burn in flame no more,

I will return to make you, weep but not in disguise,

I will make you moan my name,

Burning up in flame,

Wicked, wicked cruel game of defeat cruel game of

defeat.

ALWAYS ME

From far and wide over land, water, sea, and sky

I bid you farewell if not good night,

To kiss lips in farewell,

Not to part sea, not to make wars,

I bid thee farewells for all hope is loss,

For in my mind see you when I laugh,

For even in tears,

take you here and there,

I see you through the looking glass.

Fare thee well.

LAW

I walk a mile in the eyes of God laws,

The footprint in the sand,

I traced to find holy land,

I will not be holier than thou,

Follow the holy law,

Thou shall not,

Thou shall not,

Thou shall not,

Thou shall not,

In the desert I try to capture what hold history,

A thousand years will not replace the suffering,

Witness, burry in the sand of time.

ADORE

Adore, come close,

Comes slowly,

Feel the rain pouring,

Adore,

Feel the fire burning,

Adore, comes close.

PROMISE

Souls meet in the glow of the lights,

slide across the room,

I promise you paradise,

Just for tonight,

Don't get confuse in the candlelight,

Slow ride, slow ride,

Kisses goodbye,

Caught up in the limelight,

Ride, ride.

Go, ask his name: if he be married,

My grave is like to be my wedding bed.

Romeo and Juliet. Shakespeare

END

I wouldn't beg you to stay!

I didn't notice,

when you walk away,

I'm running high on pride,

I didn't feel the vibe,

As I shut my eyes, I look to the sky,

Thinking of you, love,

Consume with guilt,

I didn't notice how it all end,

When you walk away.

GARRETT TO ROXANNA 50

I take you Roxanna to be my wife,

you are my half to make me whole,

to cast all other aside where they stand or sit,

I will cherish you as long as I have breath in me,

to hold you from this day forward, in good times and bad times,

for richer, for poorer, in sickness and in health, to love and cherish you till death do us part,

 to never take my gaze from your sight,

 we're two flame in a fire may the flame never extinguish,

to always kiss you after fighting according to God's holy law,

and this is my solemn vow to protect you always.

SILENT

Statement to watch you in sleep,

scream,

screams bullets in the streets,

Screams, screams the fire brigade,

Screams, screams in the streets,

Who let loose this beast?

Swags and sways,

Stricken with grief,

Hypocrites of law,

Couldn't get sentence for cause of death,

While drinking and driving,

The flaw in human law.

CURSE OF THE TIME WITCH 141 -142

To endure, to love, to watch you smile,

My love and I,

I will endure,

If this punishment!

Just to watch you smile.

Be brave, be brave,

My love is here to creep and crawl.

My love and me.

BABE

There's never a name so sweet as when

spoken from your lips,

So sweet, so tender,

Waken from deep slumber,

Voice that, quiver from my music master,

Babe, a name that brought tears and joy,

Babe, never a more beautiful word,

Sing from a music master,

Drumming, drowning beats,

Lasting infinity,

Babe drawing you near, everlasting.

If you prick us, do we not bleed?

If you tickle us, do we not laugh?

If you poison us, do we not die?

And if you wrong us, shall we not revenge?

The Merchant of Venice, Shakespeare

LOVE

Love, love, the wonder of love to hold a babe in

arms,

to love, to call across ocean, times, and spaces,

to open doors to such beauty,

as to call your name,

to answer the call,

the siren song.

BLINDED

Don't think I don't see you sitting on the street
corner,

Wanting to be notice, holding your sign,

It's not about pride,

I saw the chaos,

Shoving and pushing,

Not caring if you are holding a dollar sign,

The glimmer of hope,

to bring you here in this place,

Pretend to be blind and not see your sign,

go shut your eyes and sleep tonight,

pretend that I'm blind!

HOPE

Bleak and empty inside,

Wanting, hoping you will notice me,

Wanting to replace the hollowness,

Wanting to hold what is out of reach,

Forgetting how to breathe,

Rainbows and clouds,

Wanting out, wanting to stop this madness that

is within me,

Wanting what is not meant for me,

Masquerading, as this is how human feel,

Alone here I stand, alone on this board walk,

This is my home,

This is where I belong,

Alone here I stand!

YOU OR I

Never give reason to cast you out,

Never reason to doubt the love you have shown,

Never will I understand, these affections,

This craving, this need that rise above what is my

own,

Nor will I,

Roaming on stars in heaven sky,

For you and I,

Scorching the sky,

For reason only you and I.

HOW?

How can I hold what is not there?

How can I walk when I haven't crawl?

How can I love when I was not love?

Shown the way, the path that lead me here,

How can I learn,

Teach me how to reach,

Teach me empathy, love,

Make me understand,

With a simple step I can creep and crawl,

soar the sky, I can walk!

With a simple steps with patience, I'll meet you

there,

Simple laughs.

AIR

The air at my back, struck on thin ice,

The air struck after midnight,

Kisses and goodbyes,

Icy winds,

Even in curious mind,

The air to breathe,

Clean as breeze,

To watch you sneeze and heave,

Kisses and breeze,

Get down on knees,

Not to beg please,

The air travel and squeeze,

The air to breathe.

GATEWAY

End not the end of time,

End now and here,

I see the light in the tunnel!

The end we must all get there,

But it not the end, it's the beginning,

When it's end,

It's not how or when,

 it's the path that lead you there,

to the end.

TEARS

The tears in my eyes is hurts nor cries,

It's the tears of acceptance,

Acceptance that the journey is not over,

But just began,

A new chapter is emerging,

Knowledge that I must now take forth,

All tears are not hurting, nor cries,

Not to say goodbyes,

If not goodnight,

We'll meet in the ever after,

Till I die,

If not, goodnight.

GIANTS

To fight, we must first laugh,

To fight we must understand the consequences of

these actions,

Wars of betrayals,

Wars of trust,

Wars of wars,

Wars of corporate giants,

Aahh, when the flame is burning,

We must put out the fire with knowledges,

Knowledges that not all wars are about winning,

conquering sometimes it's about the journey,

with knowledges come strength, with strength

there is balance.

PROUD

Proudly, I wear this scar!

These foundations is built on,

Scars of my journey,

Scars of struggles,

Path to hearts which is never nurture,

Scars of how it starts but not how it ends,

Scars proudly I display, this is my journey,

This is not how it ends,

Proudly to path that never ends,

II

It's the mistake I made,

dripping from my blade,

slip away from shame,

no one to blame,

Reflections dripping on blades.

FUNNY

It's funny how you make me laugh,

suddenly all the world of tears is crying,

traveling trains,

Funny how the sun makes me smile,

dancing twirling, twirling,

Funny how I'm not your number one,

Funny after kissing you goodnight I'll cry,

It's so funny my man no longer in my corners,

It's so funny how you can't speak your mind,

It's so funny you no longer bow and kisses hand,

The bed is cold with you laying next to me,

suddenly changes in the blink of an eye,

The thoughts of you near brings me to tears,

come back when I'm not there!

Thou comest to use thy tongue, thy story quickly.

Macbeth. Shakespeare

KNOW LOVE

When we love, how do we know that person truly

love us?

Do we trust?

When we cry, the tear screaming on the inside,

Know that you're loved!

See the aura, my Yin, my yang!

My love, my love how can I sing the song, my heart

hope to do you no wrong.

My sweet bird of youth, bird of paradise,

Know that you are love!

Love, love to kiss the birds and yet the bees,

Know that you're loved,

Sing the song, my lovely love,

My heart which to bloom,

Hearts radiance,

Sing the song of love.

BEAST

To kill the beast, we must first feast,

We must,

blessed be,

To kill the beast down on knees,

Oh! Weary will we be,

Pierce the beast heart,

To hear the sound, the beast fall,

The calm abundances,

We will see hiding under tree,

The sway, the calm, the falling tree tumbled.

DON'T

Don't make me be near,

Don't make me be bound,

Don't make me wear you down,

Don't make me commit the ultra sin,

Don't make me scream because of pride,

Don't make me show you the door,

Don't make me,

Don't make me want to.

BEG

World apart couldn't separate what in my soul,

Peel the layer off the skins,

I'm on my knee begging you please,

 to forgive my deceit,

Wasted time pondering about uncontrol events,

Begging you please what I witness on the sheets,

Your heartbeat recognizes the need,

 and set it free,

The crescent of which I once bore.

MORE THAN

I want more than a moment with you,

How will we know we belong?

If you are unwilling to try!

How will you know if hearts speed up when beat?

How will we know when the sun meets the clouds?

More than a moment to kiss cheeks,

Heart beats race,

More than a moment to kiss cheeks,

CREEP OR CRAWL

The breeze creep through the window

leaving fragrance of your visit,

On nightingale wing, softly light to speeding

cars,

what hope, what law!

To witness how the cradle fall.

MOONLIGHT

The moonlight holds the mysteries of the stars,

Lit the path that hold the ray of light,

Beneath the heaven,

Glorious,

The moonlight lit the path,

That led me to wonder of your smiles,

Serenade that is you,

Comes away to the moonlit path.

My voice is in my sword: thou bloodier villain.

than terms can give thee out!

Macbeth. Shakespeare

ARISE MAJESTIC

Arise majestic dawn feed the fable flaw,

Alight, arise if made by me,

Arise sweet sunshine, arise fairest dawn,

To kiss a girl at night,

beneath the moon,

Arise fairest dawn as the light touches your

eyes,

Arise, sweet, sweetest light,

Arise comes meet with such delight,

Arise, arise fairest light beneath the world and

a touch of light,

Arise sweetest dawn the delight,

To kiss a boy,

To kiss a girl comes sweetest delight,

Fable flaw of the crack of dawn,

Arise, arise fairest dawn,

Arise if this be moonlight!

DEATH

Death bring me here on the verge of shores,

Never to open that door

Death sweet death

Make it all disappear,

to face you,

Around the world and back here!

Sweet death you shut the doors,

I must accomplish, what is in the script,

You don't see me, for long and fair,

Death, sweet death,

you didn't accept the gift I granted thee!

FLAWS

Never will I cross paths, path of no return,

Where did it go wrong?

Finding flaw in the causes,

There are no excuses, trying to find reason why,

there's no kisses goodnight!

Understand this, the cover is a delight,

Finding flaws in the causes,

Crying to tears on the inside or my disguises,

The road more traveled is doubt,

Cobweb, demon,

Speak to me of hidden walls!

Speak to me of flaws!

IMAGINE NEVER

Never would I imagine it would end like this!

Never would I imagine seeing the light fall from eyes!

Never would I imagine not waking up next to you!

Never would I imagine not feeling warm embraces!

Never would I imagine frozen in time!

Never would I imagine eating broken glass!

Never would I imagine hearing echoes of inside!

Never, never would I imagine the greyness of the sky!

Never would I imagine not feeling you inside!

Never again would I allow to be unfrozen!

For this is how the mighty fall!

YOU

Words fail me, when I think of you,

Every papers I have written is about you,

Every thought I want to share, is with you!

I reach for the phone; I have no privileges of

being with you.

The world is blue,

Not to realized what was within reach,

No one can take away how proud I was of being

with you,

But it's too late to love a boy like you!

THERE IS A TIME...

There is a time to run, there is a time walk, there is a time to dance, there is a time to weep.
There is a time, we will all over come the trials, the tribulation.
There is a time when we all will set the world on fire.
There is a time, when a smile, a simply smile will turn the world into rainbows and cries.
There is a time when we will slay dragons.
There will be times, someone will rip out your eyes.
There will be a time when my voices will carry me to new heights.
There will be a time when we will face the enemy in the streets.
We will bow and kneel; you can't take away how free I'm to be!
Kneel before me and release the chain of oppression, the chain of chaos, the chains, the chain, release the chain that held me in cages.
Is this really the choices you want to make? For your reason you see the enemy is me.
To bring me to the ground, to make me cry to the evil in the eyes, take off the mask, yes, the mask you hide behind so, that I can witness the eyes that does not cry.
You will remember, the voice that will not be silence!

ONE WISH

Fairy tales and witches,

Kisses while doing the dishes,

I beg of you, Mistress to grant me one wish!

My heart desires!

To drink from what was once my lover lips!

I beg of you Mistress!

One wish!

And I will go back cease never to exist!

To do as you wish!

Into the shadow only to appear when you wish,

Before you on my knee, I beg of thee!

CHEATED

Hold me tight, I feel the tear after the big fight,
This is the moment I know it will never be alright,
How you hold and kiss tight,
It must slip mind, why we fight,
All the years erased, washed away,
It will never be alright,
Why you cheat, it wasn't bright,
Consumed with guilts, with bling, bling's,
Hope it was worth it, all the tears all nights,
Will not make it right,
Hold me tight, all the magic disappeared in a blink
of the eyes, lies, the big crime,
It's the reason why trust, can't be trust.
Becoming your bride was the highlight.
After cheats and lies,
throw the trash away,
Faded faze of lies,
Rainbow and diamond, it's not my price,
Happiness can't replace the dollar sign,
Consumed in your lies as you held me tight.

CHANCES

Are you wondering about my smile or how many miss
chances we had? My heart is big, I love a good
laugh. I'm self-conscious, I must admit I don't like
attention. I'm comfortable hiding under a rock
somewhere. Rejections bring me to tears. The
water sooth me, even if I 'm a fish that doesn't
know how to swim. Walking by the Lake and looking
into its endlessly depth, I can solve it's mystery. I
love watching fearless Ms. Mae West and British
Comedy.
I promise you will not starve in the kitchen. I will
wait patiently for you to make an appearance.
No one man love is strong for he's Peter Pan, love is
absent without a fight or compromises. The stars
are aligned, waiting for our path to cross.
I promise a friend I will put my picture in the back
of all my books. She said "Your readers need to
connect with you" I try to explain that I feel naked
with all I have written. But a promise, is a promise.
If this make sense, come find me and be one with
me.

THESE WALLS

Beyond these walls I have a life, beyond these walls I mattered!
Within these walls and beyond I make a difference,
Beyond these walls as you call them,
I see you, for I'm invisible,
How you closed your mind and eyes and unwilling to.
I just want a moment to be recognize, to say that I mattered,
I see you!
Just a moment of your time, if you will please,
To indulge in conversations a smile or a tear or two for reason you exist in thy eyes.
Beyond these walls in best and brightest will of mind.
For in life,
Rushing back and forth in best of intentions, stop and look into thy eyes only for awhile.
For beyond these walls, open doors and enjoy life once more!
Beyond these walls,
Beyond these walls there is life,
Beyond these walls, these walls for all the glory in the sky,
Like a thief in the night,   Cont......

You climb these walls, hoping to gain my trust for these
walls is build for a reason. My hand didn't partake in
building these walls.

But,
By yours words of oppression, words of guilt,
For I see you, with your poison pen spinning your tales,
Be gone, for I need the air to breathe,
For behind these walls,
I'm invincible!
Put your phone down and converse for a while for when the
battery run low,
I will be just faint memory and you will not understand,
I Am beyond these walls,
Beyond these walls there is laughter
And no evil eyes,
Beyond these walls,
I can feel all the glory in the sky.

LOVE

Consumed in love, horse drawn carriage lead the
path, doves soar,

Be Kings and Queens of the hearts.

Be true, be kind, be calm,

I don't want to look at your behind,

Imperfect the heart, my heart called you here,

Be alert, be still the beating heart,

PROUD

You try to use my blackness against me! How dare you!
Trying to push me to the ground. I will not be silence!
I refuse to give you the upper hand.
You wave your poison pen toward me!
 Drown in your lies, how small can you be?
I refuse to let you hurt me! I'm bold, I'm strong!
This lung will shout, for reasons,
For my voice will carry above the crowd
Your dislike toward me. I'm unique, I'm black, I'm proud!
I refuse to be your victim, your selfish reasons no doubts.
Put up your fists, lets go at this man to man!
Ask your self this, who will stand tall and prided?
You've entered my domain, you seek me out, you cast your
stones. Listen to my voice carefully. You think your going to
win? When I investigate the mirror, I see beautiful, strong,
and proud me. I'm unique no doubt.
My very existence bother you; you refuse to look me in the
eyes. Put your fists away, put your guns away, your weapon
will hurt me, your tongue will not be silence, no doubts. I will
not fall victim to your crime! I will fight you with the last
breath in me, I have every right to exist like you. My scars
is visible to see. I wear them proud for the world to see.
For I escape the bully who try to end me!
I witness the evil in your eyes when you pretend to laugh.
I'm here to stay strong, black, and proud.